BLACK SUGARCANE

BLACK SUGARCANE

Nafanua Purcell Kersel

TE HERENGA WAKA
UNIVERSITY PRESS

Te Herenga Waka University Press
PO Box 600, Wellington
New Zealand
teherengawakapress.co.nz

First published 2025

ISBN 978-1-77692-222-2

A catalogue record is available at the National Library of New Zealand

This book was published with the generous support of

creative nz
Arts Council of New Zealand Toi Aotearoa

Printed in Singapore by Markono Print Media Pte Ltd

For Grandma Uatifoti Fio, Mama Anasoa Purcell and all grandmothers.

E leai se gaumata'u, na o le gaualofa.

Contents

ā

Moana Pōetics

We build a safe around our birth stones.
Craft it with a dream, a gourd, a drum-made
chant.

Pile it high with frigate bird bones,
song bones, bones of
cherished names.

We rub sinnet along our thighs and lash
our cache. Our stories kept sound, where words
and names and songs are not forgotten.

One day before, now, or beyond, something
with a heart drops a hank of its flesh
before us. It sounds like a drum and we know

it's time
to undo the rope, iron-rock and bone-sand.
The stories, they tell us

that if we are the dark blue seas then we are
also the pillowed nights and days, soft with
clouds spread half-open.

We are a tidal collection, hind-waters of the
forever we rally on, to break the staple
metaphors from the fringes.

Safe.
We sound together on a dance or
bark an intricate rhyme.

We, the filaments of a devoted rope. We,
who contain a continuance and

call it poetry.

baby brother / one love

my first poetry reading was on that day
we walked to church with our teen cousins

all dressed in black + white, sunglasses, crosses, swag,
our summer seeped out of seams and ironed creases

a neighbour said they drove past, thought we were
wait-staff for a catering job, not mourners

our poem was a cornered thing in my pocket
i kept crushing the sharp angle on my thigh

so the wind or god didn't snatch it away
like you had been, one of the days before this

how many was it? those hours were steel and smoke, days
conveyor-belt cold cycling us to the edge and under—

at church they played your favourite song, 'One Love'
to tight stands of people, all pain and humid cheeks

i spoke our poem, the corners got stuck in my throat
but i rhymed it up cute just for you
to fathom your four years into a lifetime

and did you hear me when i asked
if somehow
we could still be us?

with every page i kneel
for us.

Butterheart

1983

At Uncle's house there is only an inside kitchen with electrics, no fire or woodsmoke, no umu. The hallway is always bright, so many light switches, and the twins decide that each one must be played with, often.

A glass tile wall that they thought was stacked ice turned out not to be the source of the frigid air. The air is just like that, and the wall is for decoration, even though it's colourless. Sometimes they press their noses and foreheads to the glass to see what it's like to be a wall. They must not do this, and if they do, they must wipe away the smudges.

Sina must always wear socks even though every room has carpet. Nua must nap in the beds, not under the low table in the sitting room or behind the soft dark sofa. They must not touch the plants that have unbelievably small flowers. They must not even touch them with their faces as they try to find a scent.

Big-kid cousins make room at their little plastic table for the twins to eat their dinners. They chew slowly, everyone's eyes on them, and their eyes on their parents, so far away at the big table. At bedtime, pillow space is also shared but the twins are used to this. Some nights they make themselves as small as possible. Those nights are loud with car engines and wall noise. Their cousins sleep through the bass and belligerence. Sina finds Nua's hand across a sleeping cousin's chest. They try to see each other through the noisy dark, and wrist on wrist their pulses fall in step.

Days are spent mouthing gagu and flicking hair, learning the ways of the shiny people from *Dallas* and *Knots Landing*. Some days, they attempt to tie shoelaces and fail. Other days they whine in sync and fight over toys. What they really want is a warm rock, a horse, a river wash, the plantation.

They latch on to the feel of home wherever they go: a fist of busted seam, a handful of floral skirt, their baby brother's hair.

Their mouths open to milk and bread, daily. Cereal, sugar, eggs, apples are everywhere, almost always. One morning, one of the grown-ups scolds big cousin—Oka! that's far too much. Too much butter will give you a heart attack!

The following year at school, they learn that being watched while contorting their tongues to a new alphabet is much harder than watching *Dallas* with Aunty. They stick together so the force of the eyes is halved. They sit on the grass, thigh to thigh all lunchtime, chiding each other for slipping into Samoan. Sina takes a bite of her lunch—it's a bread sandwich day again. She feels the claggy cold melt of a butter sandwich, Grandma has given her Nua's lunchbox. Her body stiffens, eyes like a frightened horse. She looks around and meets Nua's eyes. Nua's eyes move down to where her hand is already waiting, at Sina's sternum, cupped for her spit.

Nua still takes her nap in any warm corner she finds at school. She sleeps so deep that nobody can wake her, not even Sina. Her eyes stay in a dream until it's time to go home.

To‘ona‘i

We take the motorway south, going way way past
the giant ice cream at Tip Top, where we imagine
aunties in aprons taste-testing massive ice creams.

We arrive at the house and identify parked cars,
roll-calling our cousins as we launch open our doors.
It's Sunday, which is not aso to‘ona‘i, but is the day for to‘ona‘i.

We lope as fast as our mum and the warm trays
in our hands will let us go, to the back door
congested with piles of shoes we love.

Aunty Sia's laugh is like a perfectly ripe pineapple
a sweet refresh of vowel sounds—
Ha ha ha ha! Hi hi hi hi! O‘o o‘o! U‘u u‘u!

We're tucked into the kitchen by the warm aroma
of the sapasui trinity:
the garlic, the onion, and the grated ginger.

The table is hidden under food
which is hidden under foil.
Rebel puffs of curry or soy steam

sneak out from scrunched gaps.
We deliver our share into the palms
of our aunties, who kiss our cheeks

as we finish our careful task. Freed to our cousins,
we pick up play, a whole week in waiting
and games we've kept going for years

like the one where we tally all the food we've carried in
or the endless dodge ball of *You're the eldest, it's your job*
and *You're the youngest, respect your elders!*

We practise rounds of kang kang kamō,
last card and kā isu, small rituals we'll use
to sort the tea makers from the dish washers.

When it's time to pray we sneak squinted eyes at each other,
wiggle our eyebrows and stifle laughs if one of us
is caught with the flick of an uncle's hand.

Foil peeled back, savoury the steam escapes like a Disney genie.
We jiggle in line behind our mums
who do plates for grandparents and babies.

It's been a week of potatoes and budget toast,
yumyum saimigi or tinfish and rice,
boring, with a side of boring.

Not today! Today is for fa'alifu fa'i
starchy green bananas boiled into soft
bland crescents in salted coconut cream.

Today is for kalo kao,
scraped taro halves baked directly on the oven rack.
They look like pale rocks and smell even better than Tip Top bread.

Today is for oka,
creamy fresh raw fish soured with state lawn lemons,
sweetened with spring onions and Uncle Fritz's best tomatoes.

We sit on the fala spread out on the floor,
a heaped plate like a prize in front of each of our crossed shins.
I take a spoonful of oka. The taste of sea and sour is like a smile.

I take a bite of taro, the earthy bulk spreads the salt
across my tongue and I imagine that they must eat
like this every day of the week, back in Sāmoa.

Admissions interview

Epsom, 1991

The office clerks ask Mum to leave
the room. Nua looks at Sina, who gives her
the *don't ask me, how should I know?* face.

One of the clerks checks the forms
while the other rolls out a map and asks
the twins to point out their home address.

I still don't get it Nua's eyebrows say to Sina
as they find their street name and point.
The clerks look down to both index

fingers resting on the same spot, less than
two centimetres away from the flat
green grid of school.

The clerks look at each other
and shrug, like,
Okay then, I suppose.

But Where Are You From?

a 90s love song

I'm from
a diaspora gen
of second-cousin sponsors
getting 'aiga across the moana.

Panthers and cobras,
an immigrant huddle
guiding freshies
through the jungle.

Dads in Polaroid
smiles damn near as wide,
platforms almost as tall
as their afros.

I'm from
that state-house anatomy,
light exteriors,
dark native interiors,

smoked-out kitchens
and shagpile shed floors,
always clean
ever ready for inspection.

Where I'm from
Dolly and Elvis
are on the walls
        with the fam

and in vinyl
          for the fam.

Jesus and Mary
are on the walls
—on the mantle
—on the fridge
—on the piano
—on the sternum.

Yeah, I'm from
gansta rap and grunge,
bootlegged by US cuzzies,
all baggy everything (the first time around)
and the birthplace of skux.

A pātē around my neck,
Samoan Power on my back,
Starter over top
and cheap plaid around the hips.

DJ at the church hall
Speaker box in the wharekai,
fob socials, heavy suppers
R&B and reggae road trips.

I'm from
dawn fishing at Shelly Bay,
spotties fried for breakfast,
butterfish and pāua
on the rocks to be shared.

Where seasons cycle hard
from games of touch at Scorching Bay
to midnight pies at Te Aro Park,
ciggies lit behind jacket fronts.

I'm from garage parties
and railway houses
on quarter-acre blocks,
trolley buses sparking up
blazed, on the rongo tai.

Where you from?

Grandma lessons (fashion)

There is never
an incorrect hat and bag combo.

There is no harm in mixing patterns,
they have nothing against each other.

There is but one rule for colour—
wear white to church.

There is always enough fabric
to sew pockets into your dresses.

There is always enough time to fa'apaku
or braid waist-length hair correctly.

Layers layers layers!
Accessories accessories accessories!

Men_u

Breakfast at 9
a mean man de livers me from my fake broken earrings slipped off and i still have to go get four packets of smokes for Aunty from the dairy so break me fast, beat my tiny armour wearing off on my arm bent back and i hope the money stays in my pocket with the slip of paper from Aunty's hand, rothmans 25s, i hope i get her selau smokes back to the kitchen where she is baking a pie stuffed so full it breaks its own golden brown body and the gravy sneaks out to burn off until the pie is just pastry and dry meat, almost empty but still looks full

Lunch at 12
he's far from the farm i think, this kid in my class who called me a bitch because i slapped him when really i wish i bit him, is that what a bitch slap is not the slap but the person who owns the hand and uses it against his pocket-monied cheek for squeezing his chubby hands on my butt to check the dough while we were waiting in the tuck-shop line and why am i even in trouble for this, is it because the force of my slap was more than the force of his grip but my armour is the thing that clinks across the concrete floor

Drinks at 18
drown years then enter the going crowd because they all look full not awful so I rub the last fray of armour tucked in the crook of my elbow and I fake being like them but I am not in the right place and the doorways are so far apart and dark beyond, that baked pie feeling that never gets eaten just sits in the oven and keeps being and smelling and tasting like it's meant to except it's not doing its job properly and if anyone ever did want a bite they would be deep in the pastry before they knew the pie was empty

Mains at 23

when I meat him, something about white and horses and his full set of gently worn armour makes me bake the feeling that I am in need of something, something that maybe feels like food but is not food but is maybe him and he has never had this flavour pie before, for his people prefer things that are liquid and proofed, not smoke or dense dough, so he never had to go to the dairy on his own as a kid not until he owned his own life because that's how it happens for him and now he owns a car that can take him somewhere to be alone except he's not actually alone not like I do alone and he has no something smelling like something he should have but can't taste, like my crust crumbling at his lips.

Kō

You meet your lovers
in the gift, holding a fire
lit to activate the breath
of life by pressing close.

The coming together
turns a small coast
inside you
into scented folds
and feathered hair.

I do

I hang my nights upon your shoulder
and by your hip am risen day.

I swell my silk, waiting for you,
wring my salt to crystal your skin.

I shape myself into a mountain,
grind wishing breath onto your thigh.

I loan my years to fill your chest,
spend all my minutes to save you days.

I spin your hair across my dreams,
knot your helix high inside me.

I plead with stars to grow us long,
plant spans of heat in winter beds

I hang my nights upon your shoulder
and by your hip am risen day.

Prayer

for my children

Child,
I wish you warm socks
and spare change,
a bedtime cuppa
and curtains to close.

May you have
a long, clean knife
and a sharp tongue,
an abundance of insults
and a strong left hook.

I pray
you'll always wake up
and remember your name,
have friendly shoes at your door
and spare towels on the line.

My child,
I give you blessings, to your toes.
Always blow your nose
never act dumb
and remember,
call your mum.

Protection order

I will not let my pen write your name
to invoke you in black cursive
and shatter my skin-thick protection.

I will grow babies and vegetables,
swearing teenagers and stonefruit trees,
bottle their sweetness for my winter.

I will chase toddlers and foamy slugs,
dig out splinters, nits, thorns and grassweed.
I'll pinch out, stake up, trellis over.

I will not dare a pause, a rose,
something on paper to meddle with me,
poke my side and ask, 'Why so busy?'

I will dry leaves for tea and seasoning,
fuss over pumpkins and baby teeth,
rub pith and grind my own grit.

I will swill wine to empty my sleep,
smoke, sweat and sweep you under the house.
No pain, no pain, no twisted remains.

I will make mud pies and crocheted hats.
Sauerkrauted, playdoughed, sourdoughed,
tan-skinned, heavy-muscled, big-brained kids.

I will knot your name three times with cord,
walk widdershins around your memory,
grow space and tend pages, struck free of you.

Quince

Some say
it's the original golden apple,
the trickster fruit of Eden.

Downy vellus on smooth skin,
the shape of fat dimpled cheeks.
Head-high perfume, like roses.

But the raw fruit is hard,
gritty, tart, astringent.

One bite
will make your mouth take back
every swear it has ever made.

Eyes will shut tight,
blind to the trick.

She holds them in her fist,
scrubs the fur off the waxy skin.
No fear of bruising the firm fruit.

She likes that,
so easy to handle.

With a small knife
she digs out dark spots
that blight the perfect gold,

immerses the fruit whole
into tepid sugar water
to cook slowly.

While waiting,
she sweeps the floors, scrubs the jars,
bites back the urge to pray

and remembers
her own sours
she's been stewing for years.
A memory—
immersion in blessed waters,
holy words to gouge
her clean.

The trick,
a congregation
of promised warmth
and false sweetness.

Inside the sugared simmer,
pulp barely held
by a thick skin,

the only innards intact,
a mesocarp cage
of skeleton and seed.

Didn't she once have ribs of her own?

Hours
or days
or a lifetime later,
she lifts the lid.

A blossom of steam
perfumes the air
and burns her brow.

As she ladles the fruit out from its basin
the shock of cold air contracts the skins
until they crack.
Hot flesh bursting,

no longer gold
but a flaccid pink
like the inside of her mouth.

A memory—
air on wet skin
and everybody smiling
but the shock,

the cling of satin hemline
so cold that she forgot
what it felt like to be warm.

She peels the warm fruit
and a pile of used skins
slides off the counter.

A memory—
heat,
fresh pleasure

slipping
into a confession of guilt
that had her preyed upon.
She decides
to save the clean jars
from their duty,

compost the discards,
boil the cooking water down to syrup
and freeze the quince instead

so as not to see
the rounds of pink flesh
skinned and suspended.

Chronic

                         it's
                                    chronic
                           my pain
                     will bite   your hip
  suck   lower lip
  thaw   cool
    stores   of heart
until   bleeding
    it pours   down halls
    out   of darkened
red   rooms

Bitch

Yeah, my skirt is
smooth
soft
tight
and washed

coz you might call me a bitch—
but I ain't a dirty bitch.
The only dirty thing about me
are the rumours
(with your dad)

yeah, you heard 'bout me
whispered in church carparks
while kids wait in the van
and gods roll their almighty eyes.

I'm that bitch.

Painted on walls
etched in stone
carved onto boats
but written out
of rice paper pages.

I'm *that* bitch.

I'm that
thick-thighed,
pumped-up booty,
lumpy-bumpy dimpled-flesh *dream* bitch.

That stirs-up-all-the-cream bitch.

By the hinge of my jaw
their mouths fall open and
            drop
with their knees, to the floor

and all their promise is mine—
I am
their fading memory's
one   last   story
their death-row supper.

I'm **that** bitch.

That temple
that half-sleep remembering
that comfort
that punishing medicine

I'm **THAT**,
bitch.

ē

Grandma lessons (garden)

The only garden tool you need is a knife, one from
the kitchen for weeding, and a machete for everything else.

You don't have to know the names of flowers
to plant them,

we have flowers in Sāmoa this same shape
or colour, so let's just call these pua, or aute as well.

Find a shady spot outside, close to the kitchen
for scraping taro, even if you live in a rental flat in Niu Sila.

Put a stick in the ground to balance the taro on
and hang the tuna-can scraper when you're done.

Remember not to touch the milky blood
of taro leaves or you'll get itchy hands.

Climb high for the sweetest,
cleanest fruit and wash the dirtiest.

Share the best fruit with your neighbours,
even the ones who make you ask for lemons
that you always have to wash.

Ponsonby pantoum

Dad was schooled in Ponsonby,
had to carry his passport in his uniform pocket
and show the stamps to anyone who asked
if he was one of the good ones.

Had to carry his passport in his uniform pocket.
Yeah, he was just a kid but they had to know
if he was one of the good ones,
that government ink smudged brown.

Yeah, he was just a kid but they had to know
if his brown skin was legal,
that government ink smudge shown
on the way to school.

If his brown skin was legal,
like a walking court case
on the way to school
and back home.

Like a court case walk,
he had to hold his head low,
and back home
his passport grew heavy.

He had to hold his head low,
show the smudge to anyone who asked.
His passport grew heavy.
Dad was schooled, in Ponsonby.

Ifoga / Govt apology

It took a minute
to cover someone
with an ʻie toga
that took lifetimes
of oiled hands
to make soft.

Family video call

15 March 2019

On screen our faces are
like clay, about to crack.

We listen for Dad
to splinter the distance between us—

tatou tatalo,
let us pray for those poor families
in Christchurch,
with their loved ones taken.

We must stay aware,
keep safe
and never forget.

We had felt almost safe before this,
thought it was okay to be loud with our brown selves

thought we were free,
but we had only forgotten

that blackbirding and dawn raids
were hatchets roughly buried

and for decades we had let
tiny red flags sneak past us,

let our guards
slip off to sleep.

Now we are reminded
that we are minor.

A migrant shadow follows me to bed,
slips in heavy beside me

steals my comfort
warmth
dreams
prayers.

Sāsā

If we clap
while we dance

and we smile
all the while

though our hands
be come hot

will we beg-on or be-gone?

Throw a wink
take a bough

blow a kiss
never miss

and with grace
we'll just laugh

will you take it all for keeps?

Turn your gaze
on our gifts

if our eyes
ne-ver lift

Ta-lo-fa!

show you round

will you leave or o-ver-stay?

Crowns

after Kaveh Akbar

The door hinge squeals *crrrrrown.*
The child plays with little soldiers; a crooked crown slips off her brow.
Upstairs, a long table is precision set,
name cards at each place and a crown held at its head.
The meat is a served à la mode, with runny money for
mannered folk who takeaway for the Crown.
The watchful server's apron is tied in a crown.
The cat pads quickly through the kitchen, ingot eyes crowning for
a private place to eat the crown held limp in its mouth.
The gardener's crown is sweating as she grips and pulls a thistle.
The thistle yields and she shakes loose the clay crowns that smother roots.
Damp clumps of crown, cold between her fingers.
The wintered crown is buried, waiting;
come spring it shoves the soil apart to bloom inverted crowns.
The mother stares out to the garden, face crowned by a bright white window sash.
Her busy hands scrub pots for warmth and at night she coughs up crowns in globs.
A dented crown falls at her feet. How
many times have I asked you to put this thing away?

Grandma lessons (kitchen)

If you find the kids fighting in the afternoon
give them something warm and sweet, soon.

If you make a good pie crust you can have an average filling
but not the other way around.

If you want to cool it quick,
tip the tea from cup to cup, holding it high up.

If you want flavour, cook the bones,
if you want fragrance, add a lemon leaf.

If you make koko alaisa using koko pālagi,
make sure to warn the people eating it.

If you time your cook for when you want the kids home,
they will follow the smell and wash the dishes.

If you want to eat properly, use your hands.
But—

if you then put your fingers into the shared food pot
you'll get a smack on the hand because the food will go mafu.

If you want to cook well,
cook enough for your neighbours.

If you want to learn by heart,
be still and watch my hands.

Names 'n shit

Even before you know *all* of my names,
you ask me to teach you
how to say *shit* in Samoan
so you can, what? offend me in my own language?

stick my mother tongue out at parties?
just for laughs, eh?   Ha   ha
Before this, I might have given you
the story of my name

defined in full.
Would've told you that its first carrier was
goddess and warrior
diplomat and prophetess

but you won't know that now,
because   you   never   asked
so I ask myself—
shall I surrender that one, shitty syllable?

for you to spit and slap into submission
coin the term
deposit its rich
claim reward points

for your
brown-card, clout-chasing ass?
hmmm,   yes.
in the spirit of my Great Name

I will teach you—
that the word for *shit*
is how we say *your* name in Samoan
just for laughs, eh? ha ha

Welcome to Paradise!

Currency
A used boarding pass, sticky with perfumed sweat.

Cuisine
Made fresh by underpaid workers who sleep on
the floor, their tinfish dinner under a teacloth.

Climate
Sunshine. Then hurricanes
like drunks after dark, stomping around the clock,
ready to fight ghosts.

Water sports
No boundaries, currents pinch the land. Rainforests, a flood
of fermented roots.

Entertainment
The audience can watch or walk away. The indentured cast,
with wet sand in their throats—listen for the final call.

Check-out
Fold arms over chest. Hold a clock made of sugar.
Watch it melt. Turn down
the breath. Lungs like bleached coral. Wave. Sink.

1

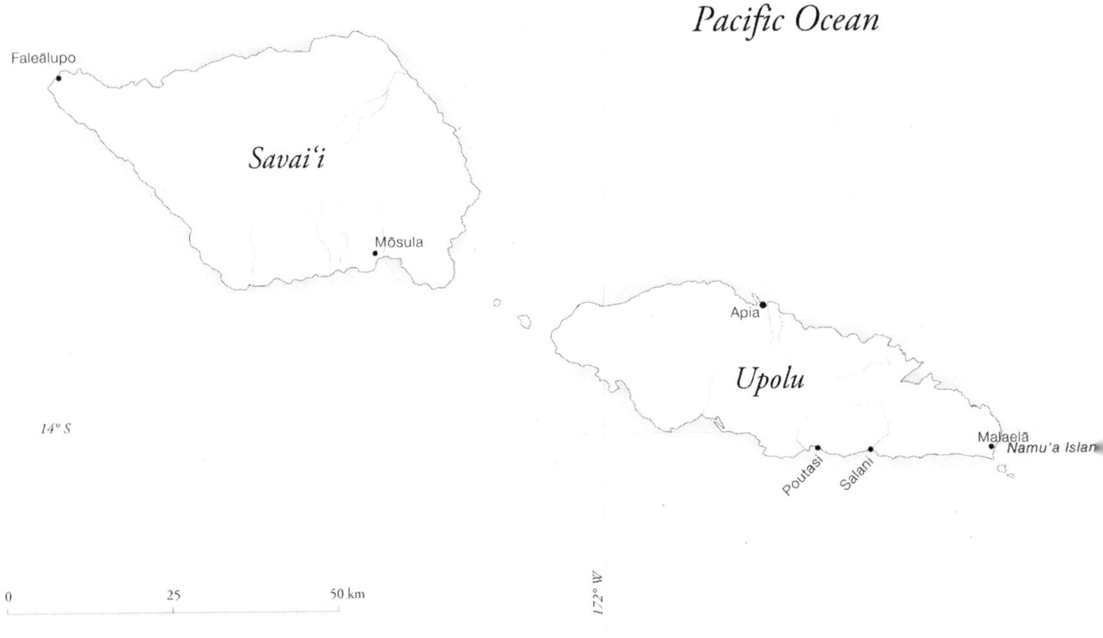

Pacific Ocean
Faleālupo
Savai'i
Mōsula
Apia
Upolu
Malaelā
Namu'a Islan
Poutasi
Salani
14° S
172° W
0
25
50 km

Galulolo | Tsunami

Namu'a Island

In the aftershock, cousin Sala used
her voice as a siren. Everyone on
the tiny island heard her—the visiting
school group from Palmerston North,
family helpers from the mainland,
the dogs—all bolted up the only path
to the top of the only hill that makes the
whole island. They faced the reef, saw it
coming slow yet fast. It broke below them with
force, fast after all. Turning west they lost sight
of the mainland, could only hear the impact.

Poutasi

The popo, coconut palm is known as
the tree of life.
When they found
Aunty,
she was
still
clinging
to the
tree.
She must
have
pressed
so hard
into the
trunk
that she
gave
the
tree
her
life.

Salani

A tidal pool
fenced with mangroves
is a buoyant graveyard
for tens of thousands of
empty water bottles.

Washed up at Faleālupo

fish birds rubbish painted timber

fale thatching a ship's bulkhead

roof iron bolts and nails

melamine plates sunglasses

waistbands and cuffs from clothing jewellery
full toiletry bags
intact suitcases single shoes, assorted sizes

backpacks schoolbooks

unopened mail
car keys
bicycle handlebars
the front of a kitchen cupboard
false teeth
buckles and buttons

pieces of church lace torn lavalava cloth

passports

Mōsula

When aid came, it went to all of Sāmoa, not just the affected coasts.
Dad offered swaps: beef bones from his freezer for tins of baked beans. Some
of his village neighbours had been straining the beans and using only the sauce.
Now they could eat supo povi and he could fill his cupboard
and belly with Wattie's beans—
cooked and canned only two blocks from my house in Hastings.

Malaelā I

Four weeks after,
I lean on a wrecked jetty pole,
look out to the pacified ocean
and listen to Paulo and Sala.

What they story makes me
shoulder the pole for support
though the wood feels too
porous to be anything
ever again.

Ua tuanaʻi le fā o vaiaso
sa fai le pou taula vaʻa ma faʻalagolago
ma matamata i le vasa.
Ua ou faʻalogo ia Paulo ma Sala

o ā la tala ua fai ma mea mamafa.
Ua mafatia ai loʻu tauʻau
mafatia ai ma loʻu māfaufau
ona o le vaivai o le laʻau.

Malaelā II

Our three-year-old
is ecstatic on the sand.
He runs bare-chested
like a small contestant
in *Survivor*.

He's found treasure, a piece
of curtain rail that he waves
in big sword swoops as if it were
a stick from a tree.

His giggle builds to a squeal
as he bounds into the water,
striking the shiny skin of
the sea with the curtain rail.

One of the big kids follows him in,
tells him to stay close and
Paulo says

it's the first time any child
has been alive
in the water
in weeks.

E na o le tolu tausaga o le tama,
fiafia e ta'alo telefua i le matāfaga,
e pei olo'o ta'alo i le *Survivor*.

E fa'ase'e ma sosolo i le manava
e foliga fiafia ma ata'ata,
e fa'apisipisi ma fa'asami
i lana pelu la'au felafoa'i.

Sa mulimulitai lana kei matua ia te ia,
fai mai Paulo,
O se taimi muamua lenei,
ua ola ai se tamaiti i'inei.

Apia, 2011

Paulo said that
after the tsunami
his children refused
to eat fish
for more than a year.

Na faimai fo'i Paulo
ua lē toe fia
tausami lona fanau
i le i'a mai le moana
talu ai le tsunami.

I dream of palolo

I spy the palolo moon
as I turn in my cold bed
two thousand miles away.

In my sleep
I am there with my mother
by the predawn fires

where we commit
to the usual ways of waiting—
cups of koko and playing cards

that feeling of stories
that feeling of
before
and before.

Fussing over knotted fibres
we test our hand nets
by putting our hands inside

and stretching
to gauge net strength
while dreaming them full.

In the dark before dawn
we're a ragged line in
the sand, scented with
moso'oi to entice our catch.

Charged with quiet laughter
we start to pray
face the sami
and sing

we hear the call
'Ua sau le i'a!'
Into the sea
we're baptised with plenty.

We scoop and scoop
from our seasonal pantry.
No padlock, no mousetrap

no tin can, no loaf
nothing to keep dry.
In harvest stance

hip-high to the moana
we laugh
loud now

swallow saliva
coating our tongues
preparing to feast.

I scoop and scoop
with my net
then from the net
with my hands

to my mouth
slurping palmfuls
of slippery green

that taste of
          salted iron
          and sweet meat
I have craved
          since
          my first
          October moon

the taste of
          epitokes
                    and epiphanies
                              to eat until
                                        we're
                                                full
                                                        on
                                                the custom
                              we must consume
                    before
                              the light
                                        burns
                                              it
                                                        clean

Moana I

Nafanua's feelings for me are
not about the feel of me
or how soaked she might get

when she rises out of me,
arriving all mythic-like,
casually between worlds,

like a name
cut with a shell blade on sand
for me to read and swallow

the serpent splash of her
the tatau song of her
the abject sight of her.

Moana II

Nua's feelings for me are simple.
She puts her keys under a rock and
stands there bird-eyed, noting empty
shells—pipi or tuatua or both.

She judges my tide but I don't mind.
When I'm low, she indulges her instincts,
and turns to where the gulls stand
in a hungus huddle over shellfish beds.

When she's not looking
I like to catch her feet with my cold
crema foam. She squeals and I let her stare
at me until her eyes forget how to read

and we both spill our salt.

Ledger

I'll make an account of our cells one day
use bone pen and blood ink, to carbon receipt
a sum split even and balanced away.

I will have earned enough words by then, you see
and with the small change of languages–three
I'll make an account of our cells.

Double lines ruled, a margin of veins
on a ream of red light where we once reigned
as a sum cut rough, two folds of wet clay.

In quickening stretch and salt mother tongue
where time goes unmarked, except by the sun
there—I'll make an account of our cells. One day.

See, there's You, Me, and She,
the inspired damp where life longs to be
but a full sum, complete. No debt in its way.

With binder clipped,
tight band snapped,
bone-bond paid
and bloodclot wrapped

I'll make an account of our cells one day
the grand sum of us
no halves in our way.

ō

IYKYK

You know?—**stama** is to man as **keo** is to
woman like **pipo** and **kgk** are same-same but
differents like **Samāori/Sawaiian/Fil-**
imoan, like how **g** takes any vowel that
mulix2 it—**le mafs** means no **mafaux2**
and **bots** is not technology but **kgk** that act
like they know everyfing about the everyfing
—and **uce**, it's depend on gender identity
like how pisupo needs **lapunda** pipo's money
—**wui**, ia gale—looks like culture can
change and language can too—**fyaku**, I'm
telling to you, **2momo** has come and we're all
seki. Jususu!

Vā: Glossary

Vaveao / vəve'ɑɔ /
is the swift pace of light
when the ao pulls away the night.

Lavalava / 'ləvaləva /
is the sun repeatedly wrapping the va
until it's had enough, enough.

Vasa / 'vasə /
is the open space where waka, vaka, va'a slide
to new places, where we become our own nova.

Va'a / 'vaʔə /
is a floating hold for fish and explorers,
how flying-fish apostrophes hold space for a dropped k.

'Ava/Kava / 'avə // kavə /
is the taproot of numb tongues and
libations to a splitting old god.

Vao / v'ɑɔ /
is where the gaps go
all dense and woody.

Vala'au / 'valəʔəu /
is the space between branches
where the trees call you to climb.

Valu / 'valu /
is an itchy tentacle of a number,
the digit points of a star mound.

Vaipuga / vaipuŋa: /
is where the river plunges into itself—
rapidly.

Vai / 'vaaɪ /
once and you are refreshed.

Vaivai / 'vaaɪvaaɪ /
twice and you are not.

Vaega / va'ɛŋa /
is a clutch of people—

Vasega / vɛ'sɛŋa /
is when those people study together.

Manava / 'maŋəva // mə'ŋava: /
is where the vā holds the mana
belly deep, like an after-work sigh.

Vae / 'vaɛ /
is an annoyed gap that only shows when you walk
flashing between the ground and your soles.

Ova / 'ɔvə /
is when you overdo it and don't know
where to stop with the vā metaphor.

Pi faitau

A fine
education is a high-sheen knife, honed to
incise tongues
over twenty-six letters.
Underachieving vowels merge close, so
frightened of glottal gaps. The most
generic fear, the most primal fear
lingers in damaged lingo, an injured
mouth to its own lullaby, pretends prayers
nightly.
Portioned, like how map lines
slit
tongue people like us. We could try to
vacillate the wet meat
hemispheres, but the
kickback
ruptures us.

ā?

a therapist asks me if I think the vā concept has something to do with why I feel like life is so far away from me right now and people so strange, and so by my logic, I should just keep moving past it all because if I am seeing life from this drone distance anyway, then surely I'm already halfway to the beyond-place they say we go to?

maybe from her armchair it seems like I have a god complex, but the one I'm named for lives in the other direction from clouds and air and so maybe I am further from her in this state and I don't feel all-powerful so what does that mean? sure, let's say it's complex.

I don't know how to tell her that vā is not really that solid a thing and yeah, we have a saying about it that gets said often to make sure we're behaving with respect to others, but it's not like a golden thing we have to chew our guts over and report our devotion to on our knees nightly and we don't have prayer books and songs about it and anyway, how is everything *not* relational? doesn't psychology ask that?

maybe I do have an obsession with distance and gaps and potential, and maybe I'm wondering what it is like to be one of the twin ancestor points at the top of the letter *v*, and what does that matter if they are joined at the base anyway? or maybe I will ancestor best like a macron, the distance extending the life of the sound it floats above. or maybe I'm just dissociated, ā?

Black sugarcane

(is a remedy for centipede stings)

A piece of sugarcane
takes hold inside
my mouth, throws it
back to first sounds.

My teeth tear fibres,
my staunched language
a moan. My sugared tongue
loosens syrup vowels.

Did you hear that? My sugar prickles
at the sound of a centipede hunting.
My sweetness, braced
for the slap of stung skin.

Every Sina from Sāmoa has bitten skin,
welts like visa rejection stamps—
one for every time she fobs out, uses the wrong
tense or forgets what language she's chewed by.

See, the syrup is no longer sweet.
The syrup is choked-back skin
like the cane's inedible black,
ripped off and spat out.

Every time I talk barefoot, I get stung.
So I camo-talk a hundredfold, like them who
crawl, drawl and talk good sting.
I cut my tongue twenty-six ways,

swallow my sugar, and still get stung
on my words, my worlds
my tongues, tense—
still.

All I have is a mouthful,
venom and sugarcane.
No hard warrior stance like *the* Nafanua,
I'm just some dust off the ocean.

A soft worrier, I'm Nua-No-Myth
speaking in centipede,
with a sweet hiding
in the dark of my cheek.

Ia gale,

the centipede is punchdrunk,
the sting I coat with sugar.

Fono ma Aitu

Erasures from 'In Search of Tagaloa: Pulemelei, Samoan Mythology and Science' by Tui Atua Tupua Tamasese Ta'isi Tupuola Tufuga Efi

Artefact I

I want to begin for Tagaloa

and the wind people who
we cannot hear inside
university halls. To distinguish legend
use.
To engage

our knowledge and dignity

in excavation.

Under
me is the

ached foundation, a near
red spectacle

an
incited
pathway

in
the
lagi or Pulotu,

to trace
inking islands.

i clear a
hurricane in
navigation
of our ancestors.

Artefact II

Early

we climbed
Pulemelei,
ourselves slabs of stones.

The middle
level is buried

meaning. I know this place,
where our people emblem the
wheke, this mound legacy
under
the sacred figure of eight.

The figure of eight pact
flows through

the pathway astronomy of
diaspora,

facing the direc-
tion

to our forbears.

Human remains
searching for

Tagaloa

Tagaloa

the

founding ancestor

Tagaloa
contemporary

Tagaloa

the consequence
Tagaloa
the

migrating Tagaloa
the
plants and trees

Tagaloa the figure
islands

Tagaloa

the chant.

Artefact III

The orator
chants the nine heavens.
When
the deceased intervene
the chant,

this invention is commemorated by
proverb.

The theft of sacred
discovery is commemorated by

the attempt to hide the vā.

According to Samoan
tradition, the Tagaloa inheritance was divided.

Artefact IV

The

missionaries

arrived as a distinct political entity

and by

colonial design

Tagaloa originates from

myth

Literally

This is tapu.

Artefact V

Colonial

man ate
this
divinity.
Core symbols

which blood
line
the placenta whenua
fanua

are buried in direct mytholo-
gy.

We return

ever bond broken
to the
forbears.

I want to underline the
means
I was
taken by.

I want to pluck some
tapu

to ask
and chant
t a p u.

Core tapu

is recognition by
the trees and rocks
rivers, and the sea. The elements
reflect on the
bond.

The

process

is lined with
essence. A
spirit
making inheritance from Tagaloa.
The
ritual,
all Tagaloa.

Artefact VI

The

ritual
account

of
sunset and sunrise

itula

tagi alisi alii o le po

faailo ao

like life and death, are
equal. The beginning of day, the beginning of night, invites

the earthly divinity
to

flare. The malae

bonfires

they mimic

incarnated

scraps of
sun

rise

Old religion,   new   reach.
Opening
the

hold,

we   search for
common   prayer

forms.

Can we place our

questioning

in   the
direction

of
3000 years ago

and
origin to
Savai‘i
Hawai‘i Havai‘i Hawaiki?

From Pulemelei

i
detect a
re-activation of
earth

mound

activities

lost

to me. i echo

search for answers.

I find in
this quest
I

accord
the world
best.

Artefact VIII

I want to legacy
for Tagaloa

in
my attempt,

Tagaloa

will

open new sight

to gather,
to heritage

our futures

and the wind people continue

to distinguish

us.

ū

Grandma lessons (voice)

Find blankets to drape over your back during morning devotions
so the children wake to a warm, singing mountain.

Find a sunny spot on the floor for your feet to rest on while
your hair is being braided, then read aloud or sing.

Find in your voice a high pitch for hissing at cats,
a low pitch for growling at dogs and cheeky boys.

Find a song, even if it's out of tune, and sing when you're ready.
Everyone will join in and the tune will correct itself.

Find a nasal drone in your singing and you will
carry the sound of all the people we come from.

grind | stone | ghost

[.]
Rest
comes in a dark box
no matter how makeshift
the grave,

how rabid the digging
of unblessed soil,
pitched
shovel over head

by a husband
whose pieces of skin
I took
as final burden
under fingernail and tooth.

>
The moon was rotted
and reborn
over and again

before our children returned
home from their school year,

home, to no mother
with no warning,

no letter, no telegram,
no notice.

It was then, so they say
that his name was discarded,
shovelled back

and our eldest took
my   name
to his own grave.

>>
I rest
two generations

                    [or three]

before vines are cut

                    [a fistful of my hair]

black sand scraped

                    [scabs of grazed skin]

and heavy stone etched
with a name

                    [a real name in brackets].

My name
peeled free
by a greying grandson
and his six grandchildren.

My name
in bold now.
They catch me in their palms
with boxes of light.

[-]
No one comes
committed to your name
or to claw grass from
where **you** were buried
do they, husband?

This lava-locked island
got to chew you whole,
suck the shadows
of meat from your
damned   white   bones.

<<
I remember the early days
when I,
freshly untethered,
would snarl over your shoulder,

breathe down your neck,
spit sunburn and skin tags
to curse you
with clammy collars.

Curse you, husband,
with a batch of lice
an excess of earwax
an eruption of pus and ulcer.

I was
there
in every
muscle cramp,
each elbow knock,

the sharp crust
of salt on your spine,

the sweat of shame
in your bedsheets.

[*]
Now, I am
a trick of light
in a great-grandchild's palm.

Letolo Plantation House

Palauli, Savai'i, 1980

On the southern side
of the biggest island,
at the sacred centre,
is a plantation

where the waterfall lives
and the rocks are stars
shaped by long-ago people.

Near the village
where, years before,
he rode up on horseback
                    like a cowboy
                              (and found his new wife).

Nestled in the front verandah
of the plantation house
is the Blue Corner,
where he sits now

with his fagu, ashtray
and pouched tobacco,
listens to Jim Reeves
and watches his family grow.

At the Plantation House
where some of his children
were born—

grandchildren now play
and call him Papa
and fall asleep under the
acres of trees he planted.

He scans the land and
strains his eyes to the softened sky,
a flock of spooked bats leave their caves early.
His son's palm-green Mustang rolls up the gravel road,
a slice of sunlight winks off the galloping emblem.

Bee sting

1982. For Papa, Martin Purcell

I've just been stung by a bee.
The whole world is in my right foot.
I'm being carried back

to the plantation house
by big cousin Losa who we call Little Losa
because Aunty Losa is Losa Matua.

I'm sobbing from the shock
and the hot sting of venom
I've never felt this kind of pain—

it's like my foot is greedy, gobbling up the heat
of every afternoon I've ever slept through.
It's getting too full to move.

I hear the crackling of stones under her feet
as Little Losa murmurs—
shhh, shhh, uma loa, shhh.

We must be near the plantation house
and I know
old Papa will be sitting at the Blue Corner.

I turn my head from Little Losa's soggy sleeve
to see he's not there—
Papa, Papa, Papaaa!

O fea Papaaa?
I can smell his tobacco rushing towards me.
Little Losa stops and crouches

and balances me on her knee.
She grips my leg and holds it out straight.
I can see Papa right in front of us now

and I squirm, trying to twist my way towards him,
then I stop. He's holding one of his
big brown bottles over my foot.

I'm still confused
when the beer fizz hits my skin,
cooling my pain.

As he pours, he clicks his tongue,
purses his cigarette in his lips
and squints his eyes.

He reaches his free arm out
and I begin to clamber
from Little Losa's embrace to his.

Papa can carry me in one arm.
I clamp onto his hip as he rises,
feel my breath steady, then catch in gulps.

The stones chuckle when he moves
and so does Papa as he puts the warm
amber rim to my lips,

and now I'm the greedy one
filling my mouth and nose with sour bubbles.
Papa's an expert at angling the bottle and

at the same time, he calls out instructions
to a group of plantation workers
coming through the pā.

Lowering the bottle, and his voice,
he starts walking us to the Blue Corner.
I'm sleepy now
and
he's saying

something   about

the best   remedy

for

pain.

in the cup

in the cup is a root
in the root is a mourn
in the mourn is an eye
in the eye is a word
in the word is a split
in the split is a rumour
in the rumour is a war
in the war is a prayer
in the prayer is a girl
in the girl is a wound
in the wound is a child
in the child is a tree
in the tree is a star
in the star is a swell
in the swell is a name
in the name is a blaze
in the blaze is a globe
in the globe is a cup

Maunga speak

Mt Vaea—Maungawhau, 1983

Talofa Whau,
I know things have been rough for you
over there, under the smog.

I hear you're barely covered now and
your crater is full of sheep shit.
What the hell are sheep anyway?

I know you might blow your top, but
I'm still bigger than you.
Hey, do you remember before the parting?

Back in our shared dark smother
when we lived in the join? That damp peat smell.
Ask the rocks, they'll remember

that we are still siblings.
You see, there are these three kids,
siblings too, from the star rock over in Savai'i.

They'll arrive through your cloud soon, on the fume-bird
and it will take no time, only a few years,
before they find themselves tumbling over you.

I promise you Whau, once they recognise you,
they'll orbit you their whole lives, aware that
the space between you and me is clear, still, shared.

You'll know them, they'll still have the smell of me
and the glint of Pulemelei about them.
Anyway, so I'm asking you dear sib,

if you could find it in your stone heart
to look out for those kids
in the way that we do.

Vaea

Double crowns

When Fuatai was born with a double crown pattern in her hair her father said: *She will be like the wind, and travel the world!* Her mother said: *Ae a! I know a blessing when I see one.*

Her hair grew charcoal-black and straight as a tuāniu mid-rib. It refused to part crisply for plaits. Her mind grew too—fast and fierce like a cyclone. If she had to sit still, as her hair was being slicked down with fagu'u, she would think and observe and flex her ideas so quickly that time itself would slink into her lap.

Time doesn't rest for long. It goes and goes and goes and only we stop. It unravelled red across their plantation one day, her father's life taken by a fist holding a jealous knife. All that was left to Fuatai was the wisp of a wish on her fontanelle.

They had to move. Fuatai, her mother Uatifoti, baby sister Uputāua and big cousins travelled home to Uatifoti's village. The children were carried like large fruit, in baskets hung from rods and shouldered by strapping cousins. For 80 kilometres across a sepia Savai'i road no one would recognise now.

Uatifoti called on all her blessings to find a way for her daughters to live well. As if in answer, cousin Tauamō visited from Upolu and the little girls would call for her on waking, at bedtime, at meals.

As the wharf bus pulled away with Tauamō and her daughters, Uatifoti ground her heels in the dusty gravel so that only her prayers could run after the bus, one prayer for every tear—*Please God, if they ever look for my love, if they ever look for my face, let them find it in Tauamō. Lord, let them hear their father's love in the voice of Tauamō's husband, Tafili.*

Antigua & Barbuda
Aotearoa
Argentina
Australia
Azerbaijan
Bangladesh
Barbados
Belgium
Botswana
Cameroon
Canada
Central African Republic
China
Cook Is
Denmark
Dominica
Ecuador
Egypt
Eswatini
Fiji
France
Germany
Greece
Guam
Guatemala
Hawai'i
Hungary
India
Indonesia
Iran
Italy
Japan
Kazakhstan
Kenya
Kiribati
Kuwait
Kyrgyzstan
Liberia
Libya
Liechtenstein
Lithuania
Luxembourg

She returned to the nursing studies she had to abandon upon marriage. Tauamō, Tafili and their shared daughters lived carefully, cradled by Uatifoti's wages. When Uatifoti tells this story, she says that her daughters started school *and flew like the wind; up, up, up to the very top of their classes—alu ma le atoa!*

On the day that Uatifoti graduated from nursing school, Fuatai snuck out to join the crowd at the outdoor ceremony in Apia. Uatifoti, white cap and eyes averted, received her certificate from a pālagi matron who had a small swinging watch pinned to her arrowroot-white uniform. The moment hung still for Fuatai and somehow, those seconds solidified in her mind, a small seed to strike a future.

Decades later, the millennium ticks over and I am a capital-city twenty-year-old in chunky heels and an oversized attitude. From the dress circle of the theatre, I watch Fuatai, my mother, graduate. She has the loveliest lone brown face in her post-graduate cohort. My chest expands like a lupe pigeon to accommodate a realisation, a breadth of sacrifice I could not fathom. I dig my high heels into the carpet and sob.

True to her father's blessing, true to daily prayers and bread bought by a phantom mother, Fuatai's double crown doubled down. Her two mothers, her certificates and cyclone-strong brain knocked the blessed wind into her life. It carried her on and on and on, into a career where time is pliant and the future is digital.

Fuatai has lived, worked and brushed her hair in all of these places. She now wears a perm, no plaits.

Macao
Madagascar
Malaysia
Maldives
Marshall Is
Mauritius
Mexico
Micronesia
Morocco
Mozambique
Myanmar
Nepal
New Caledonia
Niger
Nigeria
Philippines
Poland
Qatar
Romania
Rwanda
Saint Kitts & Nevis
Sāmoa
Sierra Leone
Singapore
Solomon Is
South Africa
Sweden
Switzerland
Tahiti
Tajikistan
Thailand
Trinidad & Tobago
Tonga
Tunisia
Turkey
Turtle Island/USA
Tuvalu
Uganda
United Arab Emirates
United Kingdom
Vanuatu
Zambia

Grandma lessons (work)

Work will be all good if you
start and end with prayer.

Work close to your grandchildren and there will always be
young eyes and small hands to thread your needles for you.

Work on forgiving the young; they don't know
what they don't know—this includes your younger self.

Work to grow whatever it is that you love
because love don't go away.

Work can make you a wife and a mother, a nurse and a midwife,
a grandmother and a great-grandmother all in one lucky lifetime.

Work to help your family. You know your work is done
when your family asks you for help.

A grand

is one thousand things, silver and green,
a thousand stories saved in a pouch of night

one thousand acres soaked in a heavy change
the smell of crusty leaves and crushed cells
the grand and great-grandmothers and fathers

who hand wealth that won't be folded or held in pocket
a thousand peaces, palmed
in helix-bound ledgers
This is what it means
to be compounding.

They Messed with the Wrong Teine

a summoning

|

Memory stays for generations.
A violence of souls
crowd Pulotu.

Above, a white ember schemes
to burn through the dark.

|>

At a city-side school in Maungawhau,
Nua naps in a cushioned corner of
the library as winter drums its pulse
on the windows.

Her twin, Sina, is sitting on haunches,
three steel knucklebones balanced
on the back of her hand. Before her next
move, she watches her sleeping sister.

Nua's eyes are marbles rolling
but she has gone well past dreaming. She's
somewhere beyond.

|>>

The village, but all concrete,
smog and refuse.

A grown-up Sina, hunted down
by people with smudged faces.

They bare their teeth,
eerie, too bright,
like stucco,
like campaign billboards.

They grab at her—
we'll have that—
pull out her tongue
and hair,
scratch her skin raw.

Language, gone
family, gone
land, gone

until they're done
though they're never truly finished.

They toss her
onto the pavement
where once there was something alive.

Why aren't you grateful?
With their arms out
they spin slowly like
just look at what we've done to the place!

Sina's guts quicken.
She rises, sprints
seaward to where

the ocean ripples
like a laugh,
waiting for her.

The hunters follow,
only their greed
slowing them down.
She's already depreciating.

|>>|

Sina dives
and doesn't stop

pain
pain
pain

her muscles twist
then release
to sink soft

and connect
with old truths
held by the sea.

|>>|<

Deeper
she hears
a dappled crackle—
lightning.

Every sense
glinting, sharp.

Deeper,
beyond the scent of mothers and babies,
beyond the breath of trees.

Hunger
comes all at once
on the current, with flecks
of food on plastic lids.

She hears language—

paʻa, their shell-armoured
limbs rattling as they ransack.

Reef fish who click and chatter,
as they plunder wrecked coral.

The echo and boom
of whales as they gossip
and bear themselves towards shore.

Human voices, trembling
as they pitch and roll in yachts.

|>>|<<

Her eyes resign their mortal sight
to stream electric.

She sinks.
An inner surge
shocks her lungs,

sharp senses
        fall away.

|>>|<<>

Under is dark   insistent   merging,
the Sacred Centre.

Sina absorbs her last thought
of lives above,

of sleep and wake cycles
now in silhouette,

somewhere distant
like fever in the dark.

|>>|<<>>

Sina has spent her breath.
The tide nudges her
back to land

where she lies,
a bundle of flesh,
eyes empty

waiting
for her sister
to come.

|>>|<<>>|

She is still.

|>>|<<>>|<

From the under place
Nua turns her attention upward.
Something has changed.

She listens close—
a deflated, cracked sigh
from cold vertebrae,

the reef broadcasts
the bubble and wheeze
of a final breath,

a familial breath.

|>>|<<>>|<<

As formless as
the breath she chases,
Nua wills her way up
above Pulotu

through dense rock
and sticky clay,
sand and sea foam,
layers of increasing life

to
the
spine.

Nua is little more than the gaze
she sets upon her sister's face.

I am here, sister,
I heard your breath,
your bones, offering.

Before she can call Sina by name,
an element sparks between them
a wide blue flash

and Nua bores
into the solidity

of her sister's bones
her sister's flesh
her sight

|>>|<<>>|<<>

emerging   merging

under   standing

|>>|<<>>|<<>>

A grainy dark,
an electric strand
of space
exhuming on the shore.

Through the belly
Nua feels an urge slide
in like a spineless fe‘e.

She pictures the
arc and twitch
of weapons
held in borrowed hands,
her sister's hands.

She feels the blood-rush
of the clot
that still makes them,
melds them,
compels them
to serve

together

as Nafanua.

|>>|<<>>|<<>>|

Nafanua awakens in the fresh spine
and stands, steady as stone.

Inside the slippery night
is a familiar rasp, eels

they
call
for
heads.

Her senses attune
to the whispered plots
of takers, far in the violence

and sees the membrane
of memories held in Sina's cells.

The body she inhabits convulses,
a splotch of thick bile sinks

into the sand, a fading green,
a sour waft.

She releases a circuit of blue fire,
eel fire, flashing staccato.

The taste of burnt metal on her tongue
brings agency to her bitter purpose.

She summons

a vengeance of rain to swell the rivers,
thunder to slap the ocean.

Together they become

bullet   knife   heat

Nafanua's cursed eyes turn to sea
as the aching limbs of the reef
                                        break.

|>>|<<>>|<<>>|<

Viral news reports and amateur videos
will show a chain of extreme weather,
unpredicted electrical storms and tidal waves.

A coastal city, streets
striped with chalky silt.

A frill of shoreline carpeted green
from tonnes of seaweed and dotted
with bloated mammals.

A reporter blinks into the camera.
Her practised face
belies the stink of rot
as she angles away
and motions behind her.

A local contractor walks
a deserted city street,
stops at a manhole,
inserts a metal bar
and heaves it open.

The news crew peer down to film
a phalanx of eels,
thickening
by the thousands
in the city's stormwater pipes.

Meteorologists hunch
over war room tables
and point at screens
and large weather maps
of complex overlapped patterns.

Voiceovers:
experts are baffled
a spate of extremes
path of destruction

CCTV captured a distorted shadow,
a figure, entering the ocean

dragging—

items
in the shape of buoys.

|>>|<<>>|<<>>|<<

The storm was more
simple
for Nafanua—

an incantation,
a flick of damp wrist,
a snarl

and it was done.

The smirking heads
of takers,
taken

wet

susū mai.

|>>|<<>>|<<>>|<<|

In the library, Nua wakes
to Sina's loud stare.
We have to go home.

Great-grandma

Savai'i, 1918

A week of sleeping
on a damp bank.
She wraps the river-
soaked sheet over
her sick baby,
her last living child.

Great-grandchild

Aotearoa, 2007

A sleepless week
before I lift my baby
from warm water,
blow their cheeks pink
and sing as they find
their first breath.

Koko Sāmoa

We meet again, roots;
cup the smoky black
pods which soul a person
to land at their homefire
altar of scales and shells
from the many-coloured reef.

We feather a cloak with spirits
clotted in your soil story,
surviving like rocks;
we mature by the moon
and return to the banyan tree
with our children.

Notes

'Moana Pōetics' (p. 11), 'Kō' (p. 26) and 'Koko Sāmoa' (p. 125) are found poems using terms from the glossary pages of *Mauri Ola: Contemporary Polynesian Poems in English*, edited by Albert Wendt, Reina Whaitiri and Robert Sullivan (Auckland University Press, 2010).

'Protection order' (p. 29) uses the line 'a pause, a rose, something on paper' which is borrowed from *My Life* (1980) by Lyn Hejinian. It was published online in *Turbine | Kapohau* 2022 and *Ōrongohau | Best New Zealand Poems* 2022.

'Crowns' (p. 46) is after 'Orchids are sprouting from the floorboards' by Kaveh Akbar in *Calling a Wolf a Wolf* (Penguin, 2018).

About the 'Galulolo | Tsunami' sequence (pp. 53–60): At 6:48am on 29 September 2009, an 8.1 magnitude undersea earthquake struck between the Samoan islands of Upolu and Tutuila (American Sāmoa). Less than 20 minutes later a tsunami hit Sāmoa, American Sāmoa and Northern Tonga. The devastation was immense along the southern and eastern coast of Upolu. There were no evacuation routes or tsunami warning systems in place. More than 150 lives were lost in Sāmoa, which had a population of only 184,000 at the time. Multiple generations of families, entire villages and tourists were swept away. Some of the survivors moved inland and never returned to the coast. Large tracts of coral reef were uprooted. Over a decade later, some regeneration is evident in the sea and also in the people. Though warning systems are now in place, the human and environmental toll of the 2009 tsunami are still apparent. After all, what is a decade to the ocean? To our memories?

This poem includes translations which were generously gifted by Folasaitu Laloaoa Tapu, Aloali'i Tapu and Marion Iosefo for performance during *Ko Au: Malosi* (Hawke's Bay Arts Festival 2023) by Seidah Tuaoi, directed by Seidah Tuaoi and Joshua Mitikulena of Projekt Team.

The 'Fono Ma Aitu' erasure sequence (pp. 76–91) source document is Tui Ātua Tupua Tamasese Ta'isi Tupuola Tufuga Efi, 'In Search of Tagaloa: Pulemelei, Sāmoan Mythology and Science', *Archeology in Oceania*, 42, no. 3 (2007), pp. 5–7. It is used with permission from the author.

Faʻafetai tele lava

To my parents, Lautafi Fio Gafauatau Selafi Purcell and Lematua Gisa Tagaloa-a-Taoa Fuatai Purcell, my twin, Tania Salamasina Purcell, and sister, Zella Schwenke, along with my brothers, Carlos Va'atausili and Selafi Junior Purcell, our grandparents, aunties, uncles and many dear cousins. Thank you for giving my life so much love and fullness, it spilled over onto these pages.

To my hearty husband, Matthew Kersel, his family and our children, Axel, Tawa, Ulimasao as well as all our niblings and communities—you make my daily life and the future so hopeful and bright. This was once a hope that we held in our hearts, now it's a book that we can hold in our hands. To my kids, you are the driving ambition for any good that I do, including writing this book.

Mālō lava to James Brown and Chris Price for your astute and encouraging guidance as well as Damien, Katie, Kate and Clare for keeping the lights on at IIML. Endless alofa to Airini Beautrais, Amber Esau, Ariana Tikao, Ashleigh Young, David Vass, Fergus Barrowman, Graeme Aitken, Jessica Soutar, Kahu Kutia, Kezia Whakamoe, Krystal Ward, Liaan Tiria, Natasha Lampard, Sean Molloy, Talia Hōhua and Tracey Syrett who were some of the first readers and cheerleaders of this work. The research and writing of this book was also supported with generosity granted by Peter, Mary and the Biggs Family as well as Copyright Licensing NZ.

Cheeehooo! to Victor Rodger and the 'Best Foods Mayo' crew: Anne-Marie Te Whiu, Aziembry Aolani, Kahu Kutia, Luka Bunnin, Jasmine Kaa, Kaitlin Abbott, Marlon Moala-Knox, Nicole Titihuia Hawkins, Rachel Trow, Shanna Aspinall-Faʻaita and Shirley-Ann Rowley for creating a safe, joyful space to write and share. Also to Ben Fagan and Sara Hirsch at Motif Poetry, Louise Ward, Catherine Robertson and the team at Hawke's Bay Readers & Writers, and Rosheen Fitzgerald and Ricky Day at Common Poets Society for always offering me a mic to jam some poems.

Special thanks to Mathew, Tina and Helena, Graeme and Aunty Pru, as well as Kahu and Sylvan for offering me warm homes to rest and write in.

Many thanks to the following publications and their editors for publishing these poems:

A Liminal Gathering (Elixir & Star): 'baby brother / one love'
Cordite Poetry Review 114: 'Moana Pōetics'

Landfall 245: ‘Men_u’
Ōrongohau | Best New Zealand Poems 2022: ‘Protection order’
Rapture: An Anthology of Performance Poetry in Aotearoa New Zealand (Auckland University Press): ‘Names ’n shit’
The Post: ‘Prayer’
Turbine | Kapohau: ‘Grandma lessons (kitchen)’ and ‘Protection order’
Vā: Stories by Women of the Moana (2021), ed. Lani Wendt and Sisilia Eteuati: ‘Ledger’
Vines 3 (EV Books): ‘Names ’n shit’

Finally, gratitude to Dan Taulapapa McMullin, Karlo Mila, Konai Helu Thaman, Selina Tusitala Marsh, Serie Barford and Tusiata Avia for setting a place for poetry in my life through their works.

This book is a culmination of so many aspects of my life, memory and imagination. Everyone I’ve ever loved has played a part in these pages and so if that’s you, please insert your name here.

E lē sili le ta‘i nai lō le tapua‘i. Fa‘afetai, fa‘afetai, fa‘afetai tele lava.

x N